NATIONAL
GEOGRAPHIC

How Does My Garden Grow?

David Tunkin

Soil helps my garden grow.

The plants in my garden have roots that grow in the soil. Plants need soil to grow.

Water helps my garden grow.

The plants in my garden take in water through their roots. Plants need water to grow.

5

Sunlight helps my garden grow.

The plants in my garden use
sunlight to make their own food.
Plants need sunlight to grow.

Soil, water, and sunlight make my garden grow.

Soil

Water

Sunlight